· Allah · Jeho...
daemon · de...
father · holi...
numen · po...
· Absolute...
Divine Being · Holy Spirit · Jah · King of Kings ·
infinite spirit · omnipotent · prime mover ·
tutelary · universal life force · world spirit ·
affliction · appreciation · devotion · emotion ·
fondness · friendship · infatuation · lust ·
passion · protectiveness · tenderness · yearning ·
adulation · ardency · amorousness ·
amour · ardor · attachment · case · cherishing ·
crush · delight · devotedness · enchantment ·
enjoyment · fervor · fidelity · flame · hankering ·
idolatry · inclination · mad · passion · flame ·
partiality · piety · prize · regard · relish ·
sentiment · weakness · worship · zeal · ardency ·
mad for · soft spot · afterlife · annihilation ·
bereavement · casualty · cessation · curtains ·
darkness · death · decease · departure ·
destruction · dissolution · downfall · dying · end ·
ending · eradication · euthanasia · exit ·
extermination · extinction · fatality · finality ·
finis · finish · grave · heaven · loss · mortality ·
necrosis · obliteration · oblivion · parting ·
parting · passing · quietus · release · repose ·
ruin · ruination · silence · sleep · termination ·

love
death

& other
synonyms

by douglas powell/roscoe burnems

Released February 22nd, 2019

Printed in the United States of America
Editor: Sunni Soper
Cover: Christopher Michael
Interior: Christopher Michael
ISBN 978-0-9998291-4-1
Published by 310 Brown Street
www.310brownstreet.com
@TheWritersDenRVA

we are just spirits doing human time
~angelique palmer

to krystal, bless, and rosemae:
it is through you i have seen all that god can be and
the divine in being imperfect. i do not believe that
god could have a gender, but if it would... it would
be woman.

thank you

table of contents

for whoever agrees

that

it is better to have loved and lost, than never loved at all.

fuck you.

try it.

when 13 of nazareth said,
"spoken word is the art of getting to know god
for a living"
what i heard was,
"art will reveal the reality of god.'

godlove diamante

god
perfect powerful
all-knowing all-seeing judging
invisible feeling glory peaceful
trusting communicating
absolute solid
love

god is love

in the beginning was the word,
and the word was god, and the word was with
god.
so when speaking these words,
this isn't poetic rhetoric,
this is me trying to get back to the sentence
from which i was created.

love.
love is two or three different, more concrete
emotions
all rolled into one mass,
combined with flesh and speech to create man.
because in the beginning was the word,
and the word was "love."
because god is love
so, i love you the way god does.
like forever, with no end,
because "god" or "love" is infinite.
and we were made in this image of infinite love.

so in a search to find myself
not only had i never left,

but i was looking in the eye of i
the entire time,
waiting on me to speak the words.
so the god in me could be revealed
this is self-love.
which is what you need first before you find god
in someone else.

so here's some questions...
like,
if god sees all, how can love be blind?
or,
if i'm looking for a true love, does that mean i'm
looking for a true god?
if in fact god is love.
or
if god is love and this is true,
why do we look up to find god
but fall into love,
when did we learn to separate the two?
or
if we "make love"
have we "formed god" in the room?
is this the never before explained immaculate
conception of god?

an intercourse of universes
colliding, planet first
emitting bursts of energy so far beyond known
to flesh and bone
that we put it on a throne;
i've only known love to be that powerful.
it changed the way i pray,

dear love, i god you.

guide me as only you could
so many run from you and mistreat the vessels
in which you are contained
because they are told to fear god
which makes them fear love
so they go through life never being able to
understand god
never being able to feel love.
even church told me to fear god and i asked
why? how?
how do i love you and fear you at the same
time?
it didn't make sense
so i had to be "born again"
i was dying to find you.

so many have died to find you.

often we are too far gone.
so far gone, we can't see where god is anymore.
this is why we look for love in all the wrong
places
in hopes everyone finds their one true god,
in love's name i pray,

amen.

the truth about god

my mother has a heart full of batteries; an
active morning leaves her drained, leaves her
out of breath. she is plugged into her bed
through most of the afternoon. recharging, most
days, takes all evening. she uses these moments
to read scripture and talk to jesus.

my mother owes her life to her faith. would
often ask me to take her to church on sundays.
she remembers all the times she's died, when
resurrection has been a defibrillator laying
hands on her. she thanks god for all her
transformations, but never the doctors.

i recently watched a documentary on how often
religious text gets doctored, how holy books
undergo transformations. i read *about*
scripture. heard there are 14,800 differences
between the original bible and its modern
version, that there's no mention of christ's
return in its earliest rendition, the similarities
between christianity and egyptology are
uncanny, most religious holidays linked to
christ are pagan and have nothing to do with
christ at all.

with this i became agnostic, not atheist. i did not
choose to believe in nothing, i stopped looking
through the pigeon-hole that is religion. felt a
huge word like *"god"* is too big to put in a

chapter book. i use terms like "the universe." i don't "pray" i "meditate." and if moses, mohammed, and jesus didn't need a bible, quran, or torah to find the creator, then maybe i should follow suit.

at a point i felt like i had to educate my mama about the history of religion: truth about king james and all the translations, religious wars, fear mongering, and the origin of satan. since then, my mother stopped requesting me to take her to sunday service. she tells me she's praying for me, never specifies what she prays for. she thinks i'm an atheist, never heard the word "agnostic."

i used to believe there were 14,800 differences between my mother and me, but when the surgeon said there was no mention of *her return*, i responded "o' ye of little faith." i realized the similarities between her and i are uncanny. the little bit of gospel i have is pagan and has nothing to do with christ at all. it was after cardiac arrest and coma left her chest split like a red sea, watching cancer be a nail in our family's palm, and the men in her life be one judas after another. these obstacles make me doubt the lord, overcoming them makes her believe in god more.

maybe she's blind. maybe i'm blind. maybe faith is about being blind and trusting what you feel

she calls it god, i call it the universe. she found it
in a book, i found it in her. i've learned too much
about the bible to believe in it, she's gone
through too much about life not to. my mother
passed down the same bible she swears kept her
alive. i swear i'd read that shit if they had a book
about my mother.

i am agnostic, not atheist. there are moments
i've seen too much to believe in god,
but i've watched my mother be god too much not
to believe in something.

scarlet

(after james emanuel's "negritude")

red was the only rose i ever loved
red was the resurrected breathing
red, "jesus speaking," mama said
red, from a book i stopped believing

red bang from the screaming gun
red, the end to keeping it bottled inside
red was robin williams' asphyxiated laugh
red was don cornelius' last ride

red flames from a tortured building
red tears bleeding the pain
red protest from fed up fists
red roar over black bodies slain

red was my first step on stage
red luminous body i became
red fire burning in my gut
red was the proud, buzzing neon name

red blood bandaged by poems
red poems from bloody depression
red pounding headache, screeching silence.
red clownish grin, face painted expressions

red is the writer who has lost purpose
red the drenching saltwater odyssey
red veins that want to cry
red the way the artist dies.

depression does a set

*for robin williams, mitch hedberg, freddie prinze
and all the comedians who gave us life and
laughter, even when they were dying inside.*

i make jokes about death
more often than i should.
i laugh.
i kid.
i have to.

you have to find a way to chuckle
when you've stacked your body weight
in suicidal
thoughts
     plans
          actions.

when all the setups sound like a death drop
you are scared to talk.
you become your favorite comedian and
it sounds crazy, but you laugh.
fuck crying!
crying is **so** five overdoses ago.
morbid humor is the new black.
more vibrant than my last depression.

ain't that the showman's curse?

colorful cast of comic relief
a prism casting colorful retort
under a spotlight
a searchlight to prison of my mind
and i am death penalty waiting to happen.

what i mean is
sad people just make people sad.
instead, here's a hilarious,
passive-aggressive cry for help:

*what do you get when you mix 13 painkillers
and a noose?*
> *rope burn and a good night's sleep.*

now *that* is comedy.
that's coping.
that's burying scars.
"better to bury than be buried."
i always say.

if you can't laugh at the pain,
then what can you do with it?
you can't load a revolver with it.
your hands shake too much.
you can't punch   line
your car into a tree,
the airbags can't take a joke.

what do you call a day's worth of suicide
attempts?

      if you do it right, you call it your last day.
      you do it wrong, you call it a looooong day
      the next day
      the world will call it a cry for attention

i have been asked,
"why make light of something so dark?"
but when life is asphyxiating
then it's exciting just to breathe.
this looks like laughing, but it's gasping for air.
a grateful sigh when i think how many times
death has been another gag.

i got one more for you!

what do you call a hilarious pun about suicide?
a real wrist-splitter.

you know what i envy about that joke?
it always flatlines.

death needs space to happen
so i have never tried to die indoors

this is your brain. this is your brain on depression.

dope.
dopamine
     on sedatives.
high is low.
low is the high.
addicted to hating yourself.

all the thoughts are scrambled.
     cracked,
     thin shell discarded and left for dead.
greasy dismay.
where your sunny side is over easy.
no matter how many lovers order you optimism,
your bed is a frying pan where emotions become
crispy and dark
and it becomes impossible to scrape you from it.
it's an abusive relationship with confidence.

an island where you lay beached hoping for
     ships lost
     wrecked and
     crashed on the shore.
floating.
     waste.
        because no one wants to be trapped
     on the sand alone.

it's an echoing plea
      in a hollow hallway
            during a blackout
                  in a now forgotten city
                        after a riot.
it's desolate's playlist:
      a juke box full of nirvana and hathaway.

a quiet cry
in a loud mind.
a loud cry
into empty and stored for later.

 "break only in emergencies"
      and always broken
grumbling to god
      but not believing in prayer.
strung out on *"why me?"*
      but never sober enough to want an
answer.

every poem is a death and a resurrection

lesson plan on conquering depression

stare. at the mirror. naked. point out all the best, then all the worst, physical or not. realize the mind and the body are similar in the sense that they are both made of clay. be a potter's hands.

cry. but do not weep in vain. hide everything sharp: knives, scissors, razors, mistakes, regrets.

build. castles from salt water and sand. pack tight. depression comes in waves. construct a strong foundation in knowing this too shall pass.

breathe.

live. even through death. lie. lie to the lies. make them believe they can be real boys someday. tell them every time their nose grows they are one inch closer to cutting the strings. repeat "i am not depressed. depression is death and i am alive. i am alive. i live."

love. be honest. be honest to love. love honestly. let honest loves, love   you.

stare. at the sky when you walk. it will be grimace and gasp on first attempt. self-esteem has been a pinched nerve. patience heals.

breathe.

create. instead of wishing for better days. wishing is for stars and children. wishing doesn't go anywhere. wishing withers and wilts. wishing has no blossom. wishing is a verb, but wishing is not action.

write. until hands can only grip pencils, pens, and loved ones. write. *i am more than vicodin and hennessey, more than nameless orgasms, more than the notches carved into wrists and thighs. more than the last kiss to a puckering barrel.*

read. the suicide notes buried like old love letters. read them with a mouthful of puns. read them ridiculous, until this blue funk can't be taken seriously anymore.

breathe.
stare
cry
build
    breathe.

live
love
stare
    breathe.
create
write
read

    breathe.

repeat.

      repeat.

           repeat...

13-year-old me

drenched in gasoline
confessing to a lighter
waiting for baptism

seconds before   my aunt
calls me from the altar

it was the first time i questioned the lord

it would not be the last

bastard and bite

he brushes his gums bloody
trying to cleanse himself of his father's smile.
he's never seen it
but has heard it was there.

he stares,
trying to find reflection
in the bathroom mirror,
     in windows,
     puddles,
     in anyone staring back.

     and finds nothing.

angrily licking the aftermath off fangs.

fatherless boys are vampires
feasting on lover's flesh,
reminding ourselves we're alive.
punishing them for being so
     human.

my mother's first son

would sleep his daylight away
and journey only at night.

like his father.
        like mine.
                and their fathers before them,

trying to find a

                bloodline.

conversations for dinner

march of 2006 was the first time my dad and i
ever grilled each other

we met in prison,
he robbed a man of his life
he was getting out in about six years
he was a man who refused to swallow his
decisions

conversations with charlton are rare

thick
       tough to get through
       almost bone dry

we chew the fat
the remains of small talk
picked out of our forced smiles

recently, there was a moment we relished
a brief, savory spot in our dialogue
where we saw ourselves in ourselves

he told me about his brother
convicted of a robbery
gets out prison in about six years
heads hung at his stupid decisions

he asked me about my brother
convicted of a robbery

gets out of prison in about six years
we talked about making better decisions.

talking on the phone
generations move throughout our mouths
and i realize i am the only one who has not been
spat into a cage

call it *luck* or *listening*
but as i prepare meals for my son
and sit
and chew
and swallow
and feed

i am doing my best to break the chain
of men who bite
and rip their families
apart

portrait

i have been an admirer of how you color. i have
been a stifled waterfall stares watching you be
so meticulous. never mixing the hues. always
inside the lines. nothing like me. never muddy
the page how i did. thank you, because when i
sunk inside the shades i forgot the brilliant
parts of me. i have been a box of gutter rainbow
paints. afraid to let *all* the colors show.

i have been begrudging burgundy wine after
break ups. a thorned rose that has blossomed
for hands that didn't belong. i was once crimson,
unrequited affection and attempted to bleed out
all the passion.

i have been flimsy petal when caught in lily-
white lies. deceitful about my intentions with
women. oblivious to the lives i've made milky.
the deception felt like pristine ivory. scared of
how blinding the truth can be. i was an almost
ghastly shade of chicken, but karma is brilliant
and doesn't stay tucked behind white clouds for
long. the more i attempted to cloud the truth,
the faster the downpour.

i have been deep ocean regret. i have gazed back
at who i once was and convinced myself that i
had too many demons to be royal. i've shed a
deep blue sea, all salty blues in rhythm.

when the tide rises, i assumed i did as well.
that's a cerulean concoction. a fallacy that
turned me crashing and cobalt disaster. and
when you teal the way i teal, the destruction
isn't as much water color as it is permanent
marker.

i have been bitter aquamarine. singing my blues
into green. envy is a wilting leaf. a grass stain on
denim. i didn't appreciate the glimmering
emerald i was, the tint of sage i was budding
into, or how my lover's eyes were just as jade as
i, all sour apple and lime from not being loved
bright. we were shards of chartreuse fading into
oblivion, fading into viridian. a pastel heart
stuck in our bices.

.
i have been powerless in my black and brown
body. forgot how vibrant it can be. how pale
insecurities want to crack walnut skin.
convinced me brown is dirty, but i am raw.
embracing the ecru in palms, the sienna in my
smile, the ravens soaring in every strand. i am
ink writing my story, using all the dark history
in elbows and knees to push. i am oak. i am
trunk and root. i am deep. i am blackest coal
forming brightest diamond. i am casket brown,
black as midnight and god. all belong to the
earth. i should have never kept my body in the
dark but sang its praise. if i knew how strong
onyx was i would have never crumbled.

i have been kaleidoscope. a mosaic of shattered,
shimmering mistakes. more hue than man

hiding in the darkest melancholy and brightest
facades and ended up blank and alone. it took
me years to realize how transparent i have
always been. and shown you clearly, what not to
be.

what you got death?! you got
depression on your corner?

i got tomorrow in mine!

deathlove diamante

death

inevitable unexplainable

frightening intriguing breathtaking

dark light slow forever

encompassing overwhelming everlasting

beautiful scary

love

yesterday, my daughter had a crappy attitude, was really rude, and got sent to bed without the usual bedtime story and song. when we discussed why, she told me she was upset because she had a bad day at school. we had a long conversation about appreciating and finding the good even when it seems like the everything is going wrong. we also talked about not taking it out on the people who didn't contribute to the bad day. lastly, we talked about vocalizing when she's feeling this way and when to say she needs space.

this morning, we played daniel powter's *"bad day,"* kendrick's *"I,"* and danced and laughed. i told her the universe is all about balance. so, because of the bad day she had yesterday, it's already lined up a great day for today. i truly believe that. getting her to understand that is just about getting her to speak that into existence, if for no other reason than to change

her perspective on how she is going to see her
day moving forward.
yesterday was a lesson.
today is a reward.

good morning.

the wake

[december 10th, 2013]

she comes into my room
wakes me up at 4 in the morn
         crying.
gets in bed and says,

*"daddy i had a dream you were shot
and the red stuff came out your chest!
you died."*

*"well, touch my hand.
am i dead?"*

"no."

*"nope, i am not. daddy isn't going anywhere.
don't you worry."*

lying to your child
it is the only love that does this
         comfortably in the name of love.
it is a means of protection.
that is what you tell yourself.
         [too many teenage nights for a specific date]

                    i awake in my room.
                    4 in the morn.
                    crying.
                    in bed

---

i had a dream i was shot.
a pour of bottled emotion
came from my chest.
i died.

i touched my hand
"am i dead?
nope. i am not. i am not going anywhere. don't
worry."

lying to yourself
is a necessary love
when you are not comfortable   in
your own body
it is a means of survival.
that is what you tell yourself.

i do not want to know
if she can tell the future
or see into the past.

eat

the first time you feed yourself
a hearty word like
                    beautiful
it will taste unconvincing and wrong.

salty,
fruitless rhetoric
still coats your palate.

eat.
until your belly is swollen.
until you are stuffed and confident.

eat
until you can't stomach
anything that doesn't feed you.

43

bitter. sweet.

i once heard...

lime used to be blue.
used to be bright.
lime used to smile when
paired up with the best the lemon around.
but lemon is a sour lover;
lemon doesn't know how to love.
lemon only wants what lemon wants.
lemon left lime for another
and lime never recovered.
soaked in sorrow's brine
'til lime became
a distasteful shade of resentment.

rashawn loved lemons:
tea, merengue, pepper.
she was an eye-squinting delight
whose kiss would cave a jaw.
the night she told me the love i had
for her would never be fruitful,
that another man made her sweet,
i bought the greenest lime i could find.
deepest jade.
jaded as i.

rejection is a lingering burn
a shot of hard truth resting in our throat.
we often need to chase it
with someone who has sipped the same fire.

we cried and kissed.
lime could taste the embittered
"i love yous" resting on my taste buds.
and, i could still taste
the night lime turned green.

breaking up in different time zones

relationships must end faster in your city.
you knew hours before i did.
you were living in the present.
for me it's like you were telling the future;
a spoiler to a horror movie
where i die at the end.

it didn't finish destroying me
until hours after you hung up.
by the time i realized it was truly over
i was already starting to decay

didn't know a breaking heart could have a delay.
i laid there, a distorted signal,
trying desperately to reconnect.

does it count as a break up
if you have a head start?

i didn't have time to fight for us.
you already left the ring i proposed with
left in a shadow where you used to sleep.

you took all the daylight across the coast.
gifted me a rotting sunset.

the least you could have done
was come back to kill me
eastern standard time.

___

46

the human body has 206 bones

my heart is the 207th

it is made of collagen and marrow.

it is hard percussion when it beats against my
ribcage

it does not tear and bounce back like the muscle
it should be.

it snaps,
      like a branch
      like a femur
      when it is struck
      by an act of god
      like lightning
      like love

that's why it takes so long to heal

                          when it
                    breaks.

falling   **in love**

you were a concrete kiss

at bone breaking speed.

i fell for
you,

but didn't survive

the

impac t.

she climbed down first

she said jump.

no.

i have seen this trick before.
been left a discarded magician's secret
a hole in one's pocket
a rabbit, left to starve in a hat.

she said jump.

no.

she may be strong enough
but is she gentle?
i am a snow globe,
and have been fault and fractured
looking glass in the palms
of too many earthquakes.

she said jump,
but the cliff has all my ex's names engraved in
it.

fuck it.
leap.

we lay there
in the most uncomfortable futon
my back has ever touched.
she held me like an epiphany.
i cradled her like a promise.

our hands said we would never leave.

and somewhere around
4:30 a.m.
i realized falling in love
is only painful
when there is no one
there to catch you.

**orgasm in french is
'la petite mort,'
'the little death'**

lunge

for years
we walked you home.
maneuvered you through every climb,
in spite of scrapes and sprains from every fall
into love.
we, the drum majors in the march to moving on,
the olympians hurling you through your
depression
like a melancholy javelin.

recently we received a memo
our job description has changed.
that we wallow and grovel now.

you've become salt-water waterfall,
heart-broken levy.
since she left you,
every day has been flow of sorrow that anchors
here.
we've become reservoirs for your grieving love,

for weeks we've been wrangled into fetal
position.
forced to stare at what used to be her side of the
bed.

us?

the steering wheels to your posture.
the ones thrusting your spent spirit out of bed
when she stopped being the cane you leaned on,
the ones who held you upright stage after stage,
the whips to your pelvis
when you became a slave to your bitterness.

we don't do pity.
we do prayer and push.
bending backwards
to move you forward.

being the mules of the body is a thankless job.
hauling around all the day's heavy
and the pounds of everything you won't let go.
you can't pacify our tension with
epsom salt apologies and icy-hot.
we aren't some cheap pharmacy date,
or some over-the-counter whores like the ankles
or elbows!
we knees were made for walking
and that's just what we'll do!

no more lying in bed
like rotting logs in a pond.
we want sit.
stand.

dance.
there will be other loves!
other thighs to touch.
just because someone walks out of your life
doesn't mean they take your stride.

we may be the stand for your globe.
but do not be atlas;
people think he is a god for hoisting all the
world's problems
upon his shoulders.
his spine gets all the glory,
but no one ask about his knees
crumbling into stardust.

every bone
has its breaking point.

the big chop

i locked my hair to teach me patience.

it
        didn't really work.
when dreadlocks cascaded down my back,
a bevy of thick cables,
they gave me power.
i didn't care for them when they were awkward
and short,
still finding themselves
(like, in my food when i leaned in to eat).

love your hair for what it is.
not for what you can turn it into,
for everything it's supposed to be

my hair promised forever (i thought),
but the older we got, we grew apart.
thinning, broken.
i felt abandoned.
i cut them loose,
but held in tears not wanting them to go.

looked at my reflection
and had to find myself beautiful all over again,

or maybe,
        for the first time without **hair** to hide
behind.

a pile of memories scattered on a bathroom floor

reminded me of every relationship that receded
into break ups.
how we were just fibers.
how i was afraid to grow alone.
didn't feel much like a sampson 'til i was woven
into a delilah.

treated every relationship like a
rubber-band
      ribbon, or
            something pretty to tie us together.
this was a gaudy love.
i didn't *adore* them,
i *adorned* them,
      like an ornament,
      like a shackle.

i was immature and impatient.
never gave us enough time to grow.
was awkward and short with them
while **we** were still finding ourselves.

love someone for who they are.
not what you can turn them into.
but for everything they are supposed to be.

how shallow is it
losing my hair
taught me to love someone unconditional.
rough patches.
no conditioner.
not realizing what you were until you slide your
palms

———

57

across what's left:
    a thinning scalp,
    a broken heart,
    an empty bed.

i cut women loose
if there was a thinning affection
i was broken.
held them in tears not wanting them to go.

confused and
scared.
callous, and
codependent.

i was quick to be
tied up, tied down, tie the knot.
couldn't imagine myself
single and exposed.
afraid the world would be too cold.
there is a difference though,
between being a strand
               and being stranded;

i used locks to disguise what i hated about
myself,
used women to disguise that i hated myself.

frightened to look at my reflection
      and find beauty without **someone** to hide
behind.

you have to love yourself for who you are

—

for everything you turn into
for everything you are supposed to be.

hair and lovers can break.
love whether they return or not.
your crown toward the sun.
                          shine.
no matter where the split
                          ends.

while you quest for your truth.
know that i'm sorry
for the lies told to keep you close,
faults of the flesh
and mistaking alone for lonely

tool

we lay in bed,
embedded in the irony
of each other's last relationships.

how the best-worst
tools to love
linger in our attempts
to hold each other
without breaking.

i am trying
not to nail you
to a poster of the
greatest heartbreak
i've ever cried goodbye to.

you,
are praying
i don't turn into
the hammer
that broke you.

drive

i showed you all my scratches and dents,
all the paint chipping,
unlocked my chest, opened wide.

exposed a bruised interior,
a failed marriage graffitied on the dash,
and a long list of drivers
that returned me
in the worst condition.

all this baggage packed
in the back seats
and you never asked
for warranty.

took me as is.
you could've wandered
the lot looking for better.
instead, you risked driving
into the sunset with me.

for that, i promise
to never break down.
i promise to protect you
at the risk of fin and fender.
i promise to hold you like a seatbelt,
to be an airbag if you crash
into a wall chasing your dreams.
i promise to be fuel for your dreams,

to run on ambition
       and drive
            and love.

if your eyes ever become storm clouds
i promise to wipe away the rain.

i promise to share the wheel
i promise to trust
i promise to be trustworthy
i promise to never leave you stranded.

because i don't want to hit
one bump in this road without you.

poems
would make a great sound track
to passion
or purgatory

my views on death and all its contradictions

i think what we mold in this earth
can be a valley or a volcano
whatever it be
it will last longer than we do
because life isn't for the person living it
i think the afterlife is a privilege
one some people try to rush into
            jump into
                        overdose into
                                    cut into

i don't always think we choose to die
sometimes we are given death
and death happens when death is ready
death needs to breathe
but lives off ours
death is selfish and doesn't check in
with the living before he takes.
i think death is a man,
because of how he takes without asking.

i think some die before they live

i think life and death are a social construct
we die every day we lay our heads down to
dream
when our dreams aren't what we want,
we resurrect ourselves like gods
from the grip of death's cousin

before she hands us over

i think the people who die stay in the dream

i think the sun dies every day before dawn.
we, here on earth, shed tears at a fleeting
horizon.
as the ones we say goodbye to begin a new day,
sunsets and sunrises are the same
depending on which side you are on.

flowers grow on volcanoes **and** in valleys
be both
destroy all that should be
and make whatever else beautiful

a flower bed
      of love
      and life
      and light

until death picks you

a bouquet for the mourning.

goddeath diamante

god
always remarkable
praying giving taking
beginning end last rebirth
coming freeing ebbing
final peace
death

lastly

cremate me.

write epics with the ashes...

shave my beaten bones into quills.

capture my last breath in an open letter to my
regrets.

and tell the world

i was

and i thought i understood where the credits
rolled until i didn't die when i was supposed
to. maybe god is the director. maybe i am just
playing the role.

end

Made in the USA
Lexington, KY
15 December 2019